Grain & Brain Diet Recipes: 61 Easy-to-make Healthy Foods that would help you stick to the Grain-Brain-Free Diet

Compiled and Edited by *Andry Brown*

Disclaimer:

The information provided in this book is designed to provide helpful information on the subjects discussed. The publisher and author are not responsible for any specific health or allergy needs that may require medical supervision and are not liable for any damages or negative consequences from any treatment, action, application or preparation, to any person reading or following the information in this book.

Table of Contents

Lunch

Lime Broiled Catfish

Pumpkin and Shrimp

Crusty Coconut-Almond Fish

Brown's Simple but Delicious Fish

Great Meatloaf

Zucchini Beef Bake

Delicious Moussaka

Tuscan Parmesan Pillows

Crunchy Vegetables with Chicken

Balsamic Pepper Chicken

Easy Garlic Chicken Breasts

Mushroom Chicken

Chicken Parmesan

Dinner

Oriental Cucumber Salad

Flavorful Chicken Salad

Better than the Best Mushroom Salad

Almond Chicken Salad

German Cucumber Salad

Avocado Salad and Tuna

Garlic Mashed Turnips

Smoky Salmon Spread

Stroganoff Superb

Mystery Meat Loaf

Delicious Meatballs

Macadamia Nut Chicken

Desserts

Andree's Coconut Macaroons

Sesame Green Beans

Cheesy Spinach Casserole

Mock Potato Dumplings

Black Cherry Cream Cheese Pudding

Lemon-Coconut Bavarian

Egg Custard

Pumpkin Custard

New York Style Cheesecake

Yummy Orange Cheesecake

Brownie's Pumpkin Cheesecake

Home-made Chocolate Pudding

Snacks

Cloud 9 Chocolate Mousse

Blackberry Chiffon Pie

Sugar-free Microwave Cheesecake

Baked Cheese Sticks

Heavenly Humus

Popcorn Cheese

Flavored Toasted Nuts

Pumpkin Cheesecake

Delicious Cranberry Treat

Tasty No-Bake Pumpkin Pie

Marinated Veggies

Foods to avoid with Grain Brain

Foods that are recommended to reduce the risk of headaches

Foods that are recommended to aid sleep

Enjoy

Grain Brain is a plan created by Dr. David Perlmutter, it reveals the truth behind *wheat, carbs, and sugar; your brain's silent killers*, according to the book, high-carbohydrate diet, and gluten are some of the most popular stimulators of inflammation that reach the brain. Consuming lots of carbs and grains raises blood sugar levels in ways that other foods, such as fish, meat, poultry and vegetables, do not. Wheat increases blood sugar levels more than table sugar. You do not have to be diabetic to suffer from chronic high blood sugar.

As a matter of fact, Alzheimer's disease is thought by some people to be Type 3 diabetes. Insulin is an anabolic hormone, meaning that it stimulates growth, encourages inflammation and promotes fat formations and retention. Then other hormones can be affected adversely, when insulin levels are high, either Decreasing or increasing due to insulin's domineering presence in the body. Having diabetes also doubles your risk for Alzheimer's disease.

Dr. Perlmutter in his grain brain book debunks the myth of high cholesterol too. The brain needs cholesterol in order to function properly. Brain inflammation is involved in multiple sclerosis, Parkinson's disease, autism, Alzheimer's disease, epilepsy, and depression. In fact, cholesterol is needed by the brain, in order to function properly, because it is contained in

One-fifth of the brain by weight! Studies has proven that high cholesterol extends longevity and healthy lifestyle.

However, unprocessed fats and cholesterol are good for you – Cholesterol protects the brain, which consists of more than 70% fat: low-fat and low-cholesterol diets also have been shown not to reduce heart disease. Cholesterol is only harmful when it's oxidized, which happens when eating a high-carb diet. Eating more of carbohydrates, even without gluten, can be just as harmful as eating a gluten-laden diet. One report showed that consuming omega-3 oils counterbalanced the detrimental effect of eating omega-6 oils.

Also you should know that the brain size is dependent on your body size. The fatter you are, the smaller your brain is. Reduce your waist size to improve your brain – The larger the waist-hip ratio, that is, the bigger your belly, the smaller your brain's memory center. Most of the brain tissue is lost in the frontal and temporal lobe, the places from which we store memories and make decisions, among other things. Once the brain begins to degenerate and physically shrink, it begins to lose its ability to function properly.

Eating foods with low carbohydrates, more fats, grain-free, wheat-free, gluten-free, and more cholesterol help boost your brain power and keep you smart, slim and healthy all year long.

We have specially prepared for you selected list of healthy foods, with wheat free, grain free, gluten-free and brain healthy recipes that is in line with the grain brain recommended foods.

Grain Brain Diet Plan- What to Eat.

This diet plan is for everybody who wants to boost their brain power and increase longevity. The dietary changes help you shift your body away from relying on carbs for fuel.

Follow this diet for 4 weeks, along with other recommendations including a fitness regime, getting sleep, and supplementation. For this Diet Plan, It is essential that you stick to the 90/10 rule – That is, 90% of the time, eat within these guidelines and let the last 10% take care of itself. If you ever feel like you've fallen off the wagon, you can fast for a day and commit again to the same four weeks of restricting carbs to 30-40 grams a day.

The list of foods below are the recommended food to eat freely in the grain brain:

Go local and organic with your whole-food choices wherever possible. Flash-frozen is fine, too.

Proteins

- Shellfish and mollusks – e.g. clams, crab, lobster, mussels, oysters, shrimp
- Free-range eggs – eat a lot of them
- Grass-fed fowl/poultry – chicken, ostrich, duck, turkey
- Wild game
- Grass-fed meat – lamb, beef, bison, liver, pork, veal
- Wild fish – e.g. herring, anchovies, mahimahi, black cod, grouper, halibut, red snapper, sardines, trout, tuna, salmon, white fish. Steer clear of any fish that are likely to be high in mercury. Canned fish are fine – opt for sustainably caught, pole- or troll-caught fish

Fats that are Healthy

- Organic or grass-fed/pasture-fed butter, ghee
- Coconut oil, Extra-virgin olive oil, sesame oil
- Grass-fed tallow / rendered animal fat
- Cheese (except blue cheeses) – e.g. cheddar cheese, feta cheese, goat cheese, Gruyère, parmesan/Parmagiano-Reggiano cheese, Pecorino cheese (the book implies these should be full-fat)
- Avocados, olives
- Almond milk

- Nut flours such as almond flour, ground flaxseed
- Nuts – raw, unsalted – including almonds, cashews, pine nuts, walnuts
- Nut butters such as almond butter, tahini
- Coconuts, coconut oil, coconut flour, coconut meat, coconut milk, shredded coconut
- Seeds including chia seeds, flaxseed, pumpkin seeds, sesame seeds, sunflower seeds

Vegetables

- Green and other non-starchy vegetables –alfalfa sprouts, artichoke, arugula, bok choy, broccoli, cabbage, asparagus, collards, red cabbage, cauliflower, Swiss chard, celery, celery root, fennel, garlic, ginger, lettuces, green beans, Brussels sprouts, leafy greens, mushrooms, water chestnuts, jicama, frisée, onions, radishes, leek, sauerkraut, parsley, kale, shallots, spinach, scallions, turnip, watercress
- Lowest-sugar fruits
- Lemons, limes
- Herbs, seasonings, and condiments

- Free of wheat, gluten, soy, and sugar

- Herbs of all types, including basil, bay leaves, chives, cilantro, cinnamon, dill, mint, mustard cress, oregano, parsley, rosemary, sage, tarragon, thyme

- Spices and seasonings of all types – watch out for packaged products made at plants that process wheat and soy – including allspice, cayenne pepper, cloves, cumin, nutmeg, paprika, pink peppercorns, red pepper flakes, saffron

- Hummus (listed as an exception in legumes)

- "Fruit" vegetables – avocados, bell peppers, cucumber, eggplant, hot peppers e.g. jalapeño peppers, pumpkin, squash, tomatoes, zucchini

- Capers, chicken or vegetable stock/broth (gluten-free, preferably homemade) horseradish, tomato paste, mustard, salsa, tapenade, vinegar (e.g. balsamic vinegar, red wine vinegar), wine for cooking

Beverages

- Stick to purified water, it is Ideal

- You can also opt for tea or coffee (assuming you don't have any issues with coffee), but be careful about caffeine late in the day.

For every caffeinated beverage you consume, include an extra 12-16 ounces of water

- Almond milk is another alternative drink

- It is recommended that you drink half of your body weight in ounces of purified water daily. E.g. if you weigh 150 pounds, that means drinking at least 75 ounces, or about 9 glasses, of water per day

- Snack ideas

- You're not likely to find yourself hungry between meals following these guidelines, but if you do here are some ideas:

- A handful of raw nuts or a mix of nuts and olives; a few squares of dark chocolate; chopped raw vegetables dipped in hummus, guacamole, goat cheese, tapenade, or nut butter; cheese and wheat-free, low-carb crackers; slices of cold roasted turkey or chicken dipped in mustard; half an avocado drizzled with olive oil, salt, and pepper; two hard-boiled eggs; caprese salad; cold peeled shrimp with lemon and dill; one piece or serving of whole, low-sugar fruit

4 Important Things to watch out for on this Diet Plan

- Watch out for elaborate dishes that contain multiple ingredients. When in doubt, ask about the dishes.
- In general, on most days of the week, commit to consuming foods that you prepare.
- Avoid eating out during the first 3 weeks on the program so you can focus on getting the dietary protocol down.
- Toward the end of week 4, work on the goal of being able to eat anywhere – at a restaurant, ask for baked fish with steamed vegetable and no bread basket.

These 61 Delicious, Mouthwatering and healthy foods, we have prepared; all which are gluten-free and in line with the grain brain diet plan will help you get started in no time. Boost your brain and overall health and enjoy a long healthy and happy life. You are free to tweak or substitute this recipes based on your personal preference.

We have tried our best to bring you the best Recipe for the grain brain diet plan, but sometimes, it's impossible to get it all right, So if you come across any error whatsoever in this book, please don't hesitate to send me a mail at Andree@grainbrainfoods.com. Your thoughts and feedback is important to me and it's very much welcome.

Now on to the Recipes:

Delicious Chicken Egg Foo

Serves 4.

Ingredients:

8 Free-range eggs

1 cup shredded string beans

I cup shredded celery

I cup sliced mushrooms, canned or fresh

1 cup shredded onions

Salt and pepper to taste

How to prepare it:

1. In a mixing bowl, place all ingredients, mix thoroughly and divide into 8 portions.

2. Grease well a hot skillet, fry both sides until golden brown.

Serves 6

Ingredients

6 Free-range eggs

1 C broccoli, chopped

1 med. onion, sliced

1/2 Cup Parmesan cheese, grated

1/4 lb. pepperoni slices

2 tsp. Extra-virgin olive oil

4 oz. mozzarella cheese, shredded

1/2 C mushrooms, sliced

1 med. green pepper

How to prepare it:

1. In frying pan, place butter.

2. Add mushrooms, onion, green peppers, pepperoni, and broccoli.

3. Sauté for about 3 to 4 minutes until onion is almost done.

4. Beat eggs with Parmesan cheese.

5. Pour over vegetables in frying pan.

6. Do not cover.

7. Let cook until eggs are just about cooked, then sprinkle with Mozzarella cheese.

8. Cook until cheese melts and serve.

Chopped Spinach 'n Eggs Florentine

Serves 4

Ingredients:

6 large Free-range eggs

1 lb. creamed cottage cheese

1/4 lb. nut butter or Coconut Oil

1 pkg. frozen, chopped spinach

1/2 lb. grated Swiss cheese

Dash hot pepper sauce

1/2 lb. Feta cheese

Nutmeg

How you prepare it:

1. Beat eggs. Add butter or coconut oil and cheeses and mix well.

2. Cook and drain spinach well.

3. Add to egg/cheese mixture.

4. Add hot pepper sauce and nutmeg.

5. Pour into greased 3 quart baking dish and bake at 350 degrees for 40 minutes.

6. Cut into squares.

Crust less Breakfast Quiche

Serves 2

Ingredients:

1 teaspoon Extra-virgin olive oil

2 teaspoons dried basil

1 1/2 cups Heavy cream

2 teaspoons onion -- chopped

3/4 teaspoon paprika

1 cup Cheddar cheese -- grated

1/4 teaspoon garlic powder

4 free-range eggs

Salt and pepper

How to prepare it:

1. Preheat oven to 325. Spray with Olive Oil, bottom and sides of a 9-inch pie pan.

2. Add cream to a medium saucepan and heat until scalded.

3. Stir in grated cheese, after reducing heat.

4. When cheese is melted, add onion, basil, garlic powder and paprika.

5. Remove from heat and cool for five minutes.

6. Then add one egg at a time and mix in thoroughly until all eggs are used.

7. Salt and pepper to taste, and mix well.

8. Pour mixture into pie pan, place in oven, and bake until custard is set about 45-50 minutes.

9. Serve hot or cold.

Breakfast Casserole

Serves 4

Ingredients:

5 Free-range eggs beaten

1 cup shredded Swiss cheese

1 cup shredded cheddar cheese

1/4 cup cream

1 jalapeno, chopped

1-2 tsp. chopped garlic

3 or 4 Morningstar Farms Breakfast Patties (tastes like breakfast sausage)

3 T. salsa

3 oz. cream cheese

How to prepare it:

1. In a medium, microwave safe casserole dish.

2. Cook the garlic, chopped jalapeno (or any other spicy addition, like crushed red pepper) and frozen MF Breakfast Patties in the microwave until the patties are thawed.

3. Cut the patties into small pieces, then add all the other ingredients.

4. Covered for 4 minutes, then stir well.

5. Microwave for about 6-8 minutes (turning every 2 minutes), then let stand for 5 minutes (continues to cook).

6. Serve after cutting into wedges.

Serves 4

Ingredients:

6 Free-range eggs

1/3 cup coconut oil

1/2 teaspoon prepared mustard

2 green onions with tops, chopped

1 garlic clove, minced

1/8 teaspoon salt

Paprika

How to prepare it:

1. Slice eggs in half lengthwise; remove yolks and set whites aside.

2. In a small bowl, mash yolks.

3. Add mustard, coconut oil, garlic onions, and salt.

4. Fill egg whites; sprinkle with paprika.

5. Refrigerate until serving.

Ultimate Fried Eggs

Serves 2

Ingredients:

4 Free-range eggs

1 Tablespoon nut butter

½ Teaspoon salt

1/8 Teaspoon marjoram

1/8 Teaspoon pepper

½ Teaspoon parsley

2 Teaspoons red wine vinegar

How you prepare it:

1. Break the free-range eggs into skillet over half Tablespoon melted butter.
2. Add spices and cook until whites are solid.
3. Place eggs onto serving plates.
4. Heat for two minutes, after melting remaining half Tablespoon of butter.

5. Stir in red wine vinegar and allow mixture to cook for another minute.

6. Pour over eggs.

7. Garnish with parsley and serve.

Yummy Breakfast Burrito

Serves 2

Ingredients:

2 Free-range eggs

1/4 cup mushrooms

1/3 cup tomato

1 clove garlic

1/4 cup zucchini

Dash cayenne pepper

Dash chili powder

2 Tbsp. salsa

Mexican cheese blend

2 low carb tortilla shells

How you prepare it:

1. Finely chop the garlic and dice the zucchini, mushrooms and tomato.
2. Pour mixture into eggs and add the chili powder and pepper.

3. Stir until blended.

4. Scramble until done, after you have added mixture to skillet.

5. Place a serving in one low carb tortilla shell, sprinkle with salsa and cheese.

Cheese Omelet with Shrimp

Serves 1

Ingredients:

3 Free-range Eggs

3 oz. Shrimp, chopped

1 tbsp. Extra-virgin olive oil

1 oz. Shredded Harvarti Cheese

Green onions, (optional)

2 tsp Fresh parsley, chopped

1 tsp Basil, chopped (optional)

How you prepare it:

1. In bowl with parsley, whisk eggs.
2. Transfer to skillet and cook omelet style, adding cheese, shrimp, and onions before folding.
3. Top with basil and extra cheese if desired.
4. Serve

Serves 2

Ingredients:

3 Large Free-range eggs

½ lb. ground grass-fed beef

2 Tablespoons minced onion

3 oz. cream cheese

Salt, pepper as desired

1 Tablespoon water

How you prepare it:

1. Brown grass-fed beef and onions together in a skillet.

2. Cook over low heat until melted, after you have added cream cheese.

3. Beat together the water, eggs, salt and pepper and pour into skillet.

4. Scramble until done.

Breakfast Soufflé

Serves 1

Ingredients:

1/2 cup egg whites

3 Tablespoons almond butter

½ medium tomato, thinly sliced

½ cup thinly sliced mushrooms

½ cup crumbled fresh goat cheese, or cheese of your choice

Salt and pepper to taste

How you prepare it:

1. Preheat oven to 400 degrees.
2. Add salt and pepper to egg whites and whip into soft peaks.
3. In a heavy, oven safe frying pan or cast iron skillet, heat the butter over high heat and sauté mushrooms until soft.
4. Place tomato slices over mushroom.

5. Quickly fold cheese into egg white mixture and pour on top of mushroom/tomato mixture.

6. Place pan in oven and bake for approximately 8 minutes.

7. Remove from oven and flip soufflé over onto serving plate.

Tomato and Parmesan Bake

Serves 1

Ingredients:

3 Tablespoons chunky tomato sauce

5 free-range eggs

2 Tablespoons grated parmesan cheese

2 Tablespoons heavy cream

How you prepare it:

1. Preheat oven to 350.

2. In a mixing bowl, combine eggs and cream.

3. Stir in tomato sauce and add the cheese.

4. Pour into a glass baking dish and bake for about 25 -35 minutes.

5. After the first 25 minutes have passed, check cooking progress every 5 minutes to make sure the mixture doesn't burn.

6. The bake is done when a toothpick inserted in the middle comes out clean.

7. Allow to melt, after topping off with extra cheese.

Serves 1

Ingredients:

3 Free-range eggs

¼ onions

1 smoked salmon

¼ cup provolone cheese

3 links pork sausage

How you prepare it:

1. Beat eggs and place in a skillet.
2. Follow standard omelet method, adding salmon, onions and cheese before turning omelet over.
3. Serve sausage links on the side, after sprinkling finished omelet with extra cheese.

Deli' Mexican Breakfast

Serves 2

Ingredients:

1/4 cup chunky salsa

4 Free-range eggs, poached

1/3 cup cheddar cheese, shredded

2 Tbs. sour cream

1/3 cup avocado, cut into chunks

2 Tbs. fresh cilantro, finely chopped

2 Tbs. olives, sliced

How you prepare it:

1. Cook eggs by poaching method.

2. Heat salsa in microwave or on stove, over medium high heat.

3. Place poached eggs on serving plate and top with salsa, sour cream, olives, avocado, parsley and cheese.

4. Serve

Lime Broiled Catfish

Serves 2

Ingredients:

1/4 teaspoon pepper

1 tablespoon margarine

2 tablespoons lime juice

2 catfish fillets (6 ounces each)

1/4 teaspoon garlic powder

How you prepare it:

1. In a saucepan, melt margarine.

2. Stir in pepper, lime juice and garlic powder; mix well.

3. Remove from heat and set aside.

4. In a shallow baking dish, place fillets.

5. Brush each generously with lime sauce.

6. Broil until fish flakes easily with a fork or for about 5-8 minutes.

7. Remove to a warm serving dish; spoon pan juices over each fillet.

Serves 6

Ingredients:

1 2-3 lbs. pumpkin

2 lbs. medium shrimp

3 cloves garlic

2 large yellow onions, chopped

2 bunches cilantro

4 large plum tomatoes

Tabasco Sauce, to taste

Olive oil for sautéing

Salt and pepper

How you prepare it:

1. Line a roasting pan with heavy foil.

2. Preheat oven to 350.

3. Slice off top of pumpkin and save to use as cover/lid.

4. Take out pumpkin strings and seeds.

5. Sauté chopped onions till translucent and beginning to caramelize in the olive oil.

6. Chop and add garlic to the onions.

7. Add freshly ground pepper and salt.

8. Clean and devein shrimp.

9. Chop tomatoes and sauté with garlic and onions till the tomatoes have softened.

10. Add shrimp and sauté until shrimp turn pink.

11. Ensure not to overcook!! Chop the cilantro and sprinkle over the shrimp mixture.

12. Taste for salt and pepper.

13. Fill the pumpkin with the shrimp mixture. Cover with lid.

14. Bake until the pumpkin is soft. Dish out pumpkin and shrimp together.

Serves 6

Ingredients:

1 free-range egg

6 (3 oz.) fish fillets

1 Tbsp. water

3/4 cup toasted chopped almonds

1 cup shredded unsweetened coconut

2 Tbsp. olive or other vegetable oil

Sauce:

2 Tbsp. lemon or lime juice

1/2 cup sour cream

1 Tbsp. chopped parsley

How you prepare it:

1. Preheat oven to 425°F.

2. On waxed paper, place fish fillets.

3. Stir together egg and water, in a shallow bowl.

4. In a second bowl, stir together almonds and coconut.

5. Brush fish lightly with oil, dip in egg, then roll in coconut-almond mixture until well coated.

6. Place on baking pan and bake until fish flakes easily when tested with a fork or for about15 minutes.

7. Mix together the 3 sauce ingredients and drizzle over the cooked fish.

8. Servings Immediately.

Serves 2

Ingredients:

1 tsp. dried dill

2 Rainbow trout or salmon filets

1 tbsp. coarse brown mustard

1/2 cup heavy cream

How you prepare it:

1. Mix mustard, cream, and dill.

2. Pour over fish and bake for 20-30 minutes (depending on thickness of fish), in 375 degree oven until fish is just flaky in center.

3. Do not overcook!

Great Meatloaf

Serves 4

Ingredients:

1 lb. ground chuck

1/2 cup heavy cream

1 cup pork rinds

1 free-range egg

3/4 cup shredded cheese

Salt

2 tbsp. Worcestershire sauce

How you prepare it:

1. Crunch the pork rinds up into crumbs.
2. Put the meat in a microwave-safe baking dish.
3. Add the cream, egg, pork rind crumbs, Worcestershire sauce, and cheese.
4. Add salt to taste.
5. Stir until all ingredients are mixed thoroughly and shape into a loaf.

6. Put into microwave and cook for 14 minutes (or until internal temp rises to 150).

7. Makes 4 large servings -- about 3 grams carbohydrates

Zucchini Beef Bake

Serves 4

Ingredients:

l lb. ground grass-fed beef

4 zucchini, cut into 1/4 inch slices

1 cup chopped onion

Olive oil

1 cup chopped celery

1 cup sliced mushrooms

1 6oz tomato paste

1 t salt

2 cups shredded mozzarella cheese

1/2 t oregano

1/4 t pepper

How you prepare it:

1. Heat oven to 350.

2. Arrange zucchini in 13x9 baking dish.

3. Cook onion and celery in oil for 5 minutes, in a frying pan.

4. Add the ground beef, cook until it loses its pink color.

Serves 4

Ingredients:

1 medium eggplant (~ 1 lb.)

1.5 lb. ground beef

1 large onion

1 large tomato

4 Free-range eggs

1 tsp. Coconut Oil

1 tsp. Black pepper

1 tsp. Sweet paprika

Salt to taste

How you prepare it:

1.   Chop onion, fry in oil until golden, add ground beef, brown, and add spices.

2.   Cover and simmer, stirring occasionally to keep the bottom from burning, for half an hour.

3.   Meanwhile, slice eggplant in 1/4" slices.

4.   Fry them on both sides in plenty of oil, until golden. You can try to blot or squeeze out the oil, but eggplant is like sponge, it will sop up a lot of oil.

5.   Line the bottom of a heat-resistant pan with half the fried eggplant slices.

6.   Drain the meat, and spread over the eggplant. Cover with the rest of the eggplant slices.

7.   Slice the tomato, and layer the slices on top of the eggplant.

8.   Bake at 400F for 45 minutes, while the pan is covered.

9.   Take the pan out, uncover, and Crack the eggs on top of the tomato. Try to keep the yolks from breaking.

10.   Return to oven, bake until eggs are as done as you like them. (Personally I like the yolks runny...)

Serves 6

Ingredients:

3 cloves garlic; crushed

1 1/2 lb. ground beef round

1/2 tsp. salt

1 cup Parmesan cheese; grated

1/4 tsp. coarsely ground pepper

1/3 cup chopped fresh parsley

1 tbsp. almond butter

1/3 cup chopped parsley

Lemon wedges

1 tbsp. olive oil

How you prepare it:

1.   Mix until well blended, the meat-mixture ingredients.

2.   Let stand 15 minutes, after shaping into twelve 1 1/4-inch thick patties. .

3.   Over medium-high heat, heat oil and butter in a large heavy non-stick skillet.

4.   Add patties and cook until well browned on both sides and no longer pink in center, about 5 minutes.

5.   Sprinkle with remaining parsley.

6.   Serve with lemon wedges to squeeze over the patties.

Crunchy Vegetables with Chicken

Serves 4

Ingredients:

1 teaspoon dark sesame oil

3/4 pound skinned, boned chicken breast, cut into 1-inch pieces

1/4 cup low-sodium teriyaki sauce, divided

1 cup diagonally sliced celery

1 clove garlic, crushed

3/4 cup thinly sliced carrot

1 (8-ounce) can sliced water chestnuts, drained

1 cup coarsely shredded red cabbage

How you prepare it:

1. In a bowl, combine chicken and 1 tablespoon teriyaki sauce; stir well.

2. Let stand 10 minutes.

3. Heat oil in a nonstick skillet over medium-high heat. Add carrot, celery, and garlic; stir-fry 1 minute.

4. Stir in cabbage and water chestnuts; remove from skillet.

5. Add chicken; stir-fry 3 minutes. Add remaining teriyaki sauce; stir-fry 1 minute.

6. Return cabbage mixture to skillet; stir-fry 1 minute or until done.

7. Yield: 4 servings (serving size: 1 cup).

Serves 4

Ingredients:

2 tsp. Extra-virgin olive oil

4 boneless skinless chicken breasts

1/3 cup balsamic vinegar

2 tsp. lemon pepper

2 cloves garlic, minced

1/4 cup chicken stock

How you prepare it:

1. On both sides of the chicken, sprinkle lemon pepper.

2. Heat oil over medium heat, in a skillet.

3. Add chicken and cook until chicken is no longer pink inside, or for about 5-7 minutes on each side.

4. Remove chicken to a serving platter and keep it warm.

5. Mix broth, vinegar, and garlic and add to the skillet.

6. Stir cook over medium-high heat until the mixture is reduced and slightly thickened, or for about 2 minutes. Pour sauce over chicken breasts and serve.

Tip: You can double the sauce ingredients if you want extra sauce for dipping.

Easy Garlic Chicken Breasts

Serves 2

Ingredients:

1/4 cup lime juice

1 Tbsp. minced garlic

1/4 cup Extra-virgin olive oil

Salt and pepper

2 boneless, skinless chicken breasts

How you prepare it:

1. In a medium bowl, whisk together the olive oil and lime juice.

2. Add garlic and season with salt and pepper generously, and add chicken, making sure it is well-coated with the marinade.

3. Marinate chicken, covered in fridge preferably overnight or for at least 3 hours.

4. Preheat oven to 400 degrees F.

5. Discard marinade, after removing chicken from marinade.

6. In a shallow baking pan, arrange chicken breasts.

7. Season with salt and pepper and roast until chicken is cooked through for about 25-30 minutes and the juices run clear when you prick it with a fork.

Note: This recipe is really simple, but surprisingly good. The chicken is somewhat garlicky and tangy because of the lime juice, but it is not too strong-tasting.

Mushroom Chicken

Serves 6

Ingredients:

12 chicken thighs

Paprika

Salt and Pepper

Sauce:

1/2 pound mushrooms, sliced

1/4 cup butter

3/4 cup whipping cream

1 tbsp. almond flour

1 tsp. soy sauce

How you prepare it:

1. Preheat oven to 350 F.

2. On a rack over a large cookie sheet, place chicken thighs.

3. Season with salt and pepper to taste. Generously dust with paprika.

4. Bake for 1 hr. To make sauce, melt butter in large skillet.

5. Add mushrooms; sprinkle with flour, toss mushrooms to distribute flour.

6. Sauté over medium heat, stirring occasionally for 8 to 10 minutes.

7. Add soy sauce, and slowly stir in cream.

8. Cook and stir till mixture bubbles and thickens.

9. Season to taste with salt and pepper.

10. Serve over baked chicken thighs.

Serves 4

Ingredients:

1 egg, slightly beaten

4 boneless and skinless chicken breast halves

1/2 cup crushed pork rinds

1/2 cup tomato sauce

2 tbsp. Almond butter

1/2 cup Shredded mozzarella cheese

1/4 cup Chopped fresh parsley

1 tbsp. Grated Parmesan cheese

How you prepare it:

1. Flatten chicken to even thickness, using palm of hand.

2. Dip chicken into egg then into crumbs to coat.

3. In skillet over medium heat, in hot margarine, brown chicken on both sides.

4. Add tomato sauce. Reduce heat. Cover; simmer 10 minutes.

5. Sprinkle with cheeses and parsley. Cover; simmer until cheese melts, about 5 minutes.

Oriental Cucumber Salad

Serves 4

Ingredients:

1/4 teaspoon Extra-virgin olive oil

2 tablespoons seasoned rice vinegar

1/4 teaspoon salt

1/2 small red onion, thinly sliced

1 English (seedless) cucumber (about 12 ounces), unpeeled and thinly sliced

How you prepare it:

1. In medium bowl, with wire whisk, salt, mix vinegar, and sesame oil until blended.
2. Add red onion, and cucumber and toss to coat.

Flavorful Chicken Salad

Serves 2

Ingredients:

1/4 cup sliced mushrooms

1 cup cooked chicken breast, shredded

2 cups lettuce, shredded

2 Tbsp. green onion, minced

1 cup sweet red pepper, diced

1/4 cup almond butter

1 tsp. salt

1/2 cup mozzarella cheese, shredded

1 Tbsp. lemon juice

How you prepare it:

1. Mix the mushrooms, chicken, almond butter, lemon juice, peppers, green and herbal blend, in a large bowl.

2. Coat a small baking sheet with non-stick spray. Form the chicken mixture into 2 flat patties.

3. Place on the sheet. Sprinkle the chicken mixture with the mozzarella.

4. Place in the broiler, and broil about 4 inches from the heat until the cheese has melted and the chicken is warmed through, about 5 minutes.

5. Place the lettuce on two dinner plates.

6. Garnish with the lemon slices and Top with the hot chicken mixture. Makes 2 servings.

Serves 6

Ingredients:

1/2 pound mushroom

1 tbsp. Extra-virgin olive oil

1 tsp. basil and marjoram

3 cloves garlic, chopped fine

1 medium tomato, diced

3 tablespoons lemon juice

1 pinch fresh ground pepper

1/2 cup water

1 tablespoon fresh chopped parsley or fresh coriander

1 pinch salt

How you prepare it:

1. Heat the oil on low in a frying pan, then gently fry the mushrooms for 2-3 minutes.

2. Do not overcook. Sprinkle in basil and garlic, then toss the mixture so that mushrooms are well coated for a minute or two.

3. Add the lemon juice, salt, water, tomato, and pepper.

4. Stir together and cook until the tomato softens.

5. Remove from heat and let cool.

6. Garnish with chopped herbs.

Almond Chicken Salad

Serves 4-6

Ingredients:

4 cups cubed cooked chicken

1 cup chopped celery

1 1/2 cups seedless green grapes

3/4 cup sliced green onion

3 free-range eggs, chopped

1/2 cup almond butter

1/2 tsp. pepper

1/4 cup sour cream

1 Tbsp. prepared mustard

1 tsp. salt

1/4 tsp. onion pepper

1/4 tsp. celery salt

1/8 tsp. dry mustard

1/8 tsp. paprika

1 kiwifruit, peeled and sliced (optional)

1/2 cup slivered almonds, toasted

How you prepare it:

1. Combine grapes, celery, onions, chicken, and eggs, in large bowl.

2. Combine the other nine ingredients, in another bowl; stir until smooth.

3. Pour over chicken mixture and toss gently.

4. Stir in almonds and serve immediately, or refrigerate and add almonds right before serving.

5. Garnish with kiwifruit if desired.

German Cucumber Salad

Serves 6

Ingredients:

2 cucumbers, thinly sliced

4 green onions, thinly sliced

3 small tomatoes

1/4 cup sour cream

1/4 Teaspoon mustard

1/2 Teaspoon pepper

2 Tablespoons minced dill

2 Tablespoons snipped parsley

1 Tablespoon vinegar

1 Tablespoon heavy cream

1/2 Teaspoon salt

How you prepare it:

1. Dice and combine onions, tomatoes, cucumbers and parsley.

2. Combine dressing ingredients separately then pour over salad and toss lightly.

3. Before serving, chill at least 1 hour.

Serves 4

Ingredients:

2 Teaspoons hot sauce

2 large hard boiled eggs

1/2 cup onion, chopped

1 can tuna

1 cup avocado, mashed

2 Tablespoons almond butter

Fresh lemon juice

2 Tablespoons pickle relish

Salt, to taste

How you prepare it:

1. Peel eggs and mince with dinner fork.

2. To prevent discoloration, peel avocado and squeeze on half lemon juice.

3. Mash avocado in with egg.

4. Drain tuna and mix into egg/avocado, adding onions, relish, almond butter, salt and hot sauce.

5. Stir well and serve over a bed of fresh lettuce.

Garlic Mashed Turnips

Serves 4

Ingredients:

1/4 cup heavy cream

3 cups diced turnip

2 cloves garlic, minced

3 T melted Almond butter

Salt, pepper

How you prepare it:

1. Boil turnips until tender.

2. Drain and mash turnips as you would for mashed potatoes.

3. Stir in heavy cream, salt, butter, pepper and garlic.

4. If you prefer to blend until smooth, use food processor.

Smoky Salmon Spread

Serves 4

Ingredients:

2 8-oz packages cream cheese

2 6-oz cans boneless, skinless pink salmon

3 Tbs. lemon juice

1 tsp. dill weed

3 Tbs. cream

3-4 drops liquid smoke flavoring

Pork skins

1/4 cup green onions

How you prepare it:

1. Drain salmon. Beat cream cheese with lemon juice, cream and dill weed in mixer until light and fluffy.

2. Beat in green onions and salmon until thoroughly combined.

3. Season with liquid smoke to taste.

4. Before serving, chill several hours to allow flavors to blend.

5. Spread on pork skins, to serve.

Serves 2

Ingredients:

1/2 cup chopped onion

1 pound grass-fed beef or beef sirloin steak, cut into thin strips

3 Tablespoons real butter

1 4-ounce can mushrooms, drained

1/2 teaspoon salt

1/4 teaspoon pepper

4 oz. Cream Cheese, cubed

1/4 teaspoon dry mustard

4 oz. Sour Cream

1/3 cup water

1/3 cup heavy cream

How you prepare it:

1. In large skillet, brown beef in butter.

2. Add mushrooms, onions, and seasoning, cook until vegetables are tender.

3. Add cream cheese, milk, sour cream and water; stir over low heat until cream cheese is melted.

4. Eat as it! Or Serve over your favorite noodle substitute.

Mystery Meat Loaf

Serves 6

Ingredients:

Garlic salt, to taste

3 pounds ground grass-fed beef

Seasoned pepper, to taste

4 to 6 large eggs, hard boiled

Chopped parsley

1 (16-ounce) can tomato sauce

Seasoned salt, to taste

How you prepare it:

1. Preheat oven to 350 degrees.
2. Mix together ground grass-fed beef, in a large bowl seasoned salt and pepper and garlic salt to taste.
3. In the bottom of a 13*9-inch Pyrex pan form half meat mixture into a free form or oval shape.

4. Place eggs end to end across meat lengthways.

5. Arrange remaining half meat covering eggs.

6. Score meat all the way around, with a fork.

7. Pour tomato sauce over top and around meat loaf.

8. Sprinkle with chopped parsley.

9. Bake for one and a half hours, cut into slices and serve.

<u>**Serves 6**</u>

Ingredients:

1 pound ground beef

1/4 cup Almond Milk

1 large free-range egg

3/4 teaspoon salt

1/4 cup onion, chopped

1/8 teaspoon pepper

1 tsp. Worcestershire Sauce

1/3 cup crushed pork rinds

How you prepare it:

1. Mix all the ingredients together.
2. Shape mixture by Tablespoonful into one 1" balls.
3. Place the meatballs in a lightly greased baking pan and bake, until light brown, about 20 minutes uncovered, in a 400~ oven.
4. Drain off the excess fat.

Macadamia Nut Chicken

Serves 4

Ingredients:

1 free-range egg

4-6 chicken or fish cutlets

1 cup Macadamia nut crumbs

1/2 cup Macadamia nut oil (or an olive oil/butter combination)

2 tbsp. lemon juice

Fresh chopped parsley

Salt and pepper

How you prepare it:

1. Dry the roll and cutlets in seasoned flour.
2. Cover cutlets with beaten free-range egg and roll in Macadamia nut crumbs.
3. Heat oil in pan and fry cutlets gently until light brown either side.

4. Add lemon juice and continue cooking for 5 minutes.

5. Serve garnished with parsley.

Andree's Coconut Macaroons

Ingredients:

1/2 cup free-range egg, beaten

2 1/2 cups unsweetened moist shredded coconut

Stevia sweetener as Desired

1/2 tsp. vanilla extract

1/4 tsp. salt

How you prepare it:

1. Beat the free-range egg until fluffy but not stiff.

2. Stir in salt, sweetener, vanilla.

3. Blend in coconut. Serve

4. This Recipe makes about 30 cookies. Bake at 325 about 15 to 20 minutes, or until lightly browned.

Notes: This cookies are healthy and are gluten-free, so no worries. I've seen unsweetened coconut either in the frozen fruit area, or in bulk bins, but never in the regular baking aisle. Mine from the bulk bins is pretty dry, and the first time I made the recipe, it came out rather dry, so when I made my second batch, I mixed the 2 1/2 cups of dry coconut with about 1/2 cup water and let it sit in the fridge a little while before making the recipe.

Sesame Green Beans

Serves 6

Ingredients:

3/4 pound fresh green beans

1/2 cup water

1 Tablespoon Almond butter

1 Tablespoon soy sauce

2 teaspoons of sesame seeds, toasted

How you prepare it:

1. In a saucepan, bring beans and water to a boil; reduce heat to medium.

2. Cover and cook until the beans are crisp-tender, for about 10-15 minutes; drain.

3. Add soy sauce, butter, and sesame seeds; toss to coat.

Cheesy Spinach Casserole

Serves 4

Ingredients:

3 oz. cream cheese

2 10-oz. packages frozen chopped spinach

1/4 c. Almond butter

1/4 c. Parmesan cheese

1/2 c. pecans, chopped (walnuts work well too)

Salt and pepper

How you prepare it:

1. Cook spinach in salted water. Drain.

2. Melt butter and cream cheese together and add to spinach.

3. Put in casserole dish.

4. Top with pecans and parmesan.

5. Heat at 350 degrees.

6. Serve Immediately.

Mock Potato Dumplings

Serves 2

Ingredients:

2 free-range eggs, beaten

1/2 head cauliflower (1 cup mashed)

1/2 cup grated Parmesan cheese

1 tsp. nutmeg

1 tsp. parsley

4 T soy flour

4 T butter

1 T salt

How you prepare it:

1. Boil cauliflower for about 25 minutes until soft. (I like to boil mine in chicken broth, makes it more flavorful)

2. Drain water and mash with fork or potato masher.

3. Add Parmesan cheese, eggs, nutmeg, and parsley and soy flour.

4. Shape into walnut-size balls.

5. Bring large pot of water to rolling boil. Add salt.

6. Drop cauliflower dumplings into water.

7. When they rise, remove with slotted spoon.

8. Heat butter in skillet.

9. Fry dumplings until brown on all sides.

10.   Drain on paper towel.

Black Cherry Cream Cheese Pudding

Serves 2

Ingredients:

1/2 Cup cream

1 Free-range egg

3 Tbsp. Stevia (heaping)

1 prepared snack-size Jell-O brand Black Cherry sugar-free gelatin dessert

1 tsp. vanilla

How you prepare it:

1. In a mixing bowl, blend all six ingredients and then whip on high speed until smooth and fluffy. The fluffier the better.
2. Pour it into a small shallow casserole dish and bake uncovered at 400° F for 30 minutes, until mixture has a skin on top and doesn't look like it would pour out of the dish easily.
3. Remove from oven and let cool. Refrigerate for 2 hours.
4. Spoon into serving dishes.

5. It's great, by the way. The black cherry Jello, liquefied by the heat of the oven, re-gels on the bottom of the dish during refrigeration. I loved it!

Lemon-Coconut Bavarian

Serves 4

Ingredients:

1 12-oz can of coconut milk

1/2 cup unsweetened coconut flakes

1 tsp coconut extract

1 box SF Lemon Jell-O

1 pkg. Knox's unflavored gelatin

1 cup boiling water

4 ice cubes

1 tbsp. Stevia sweetener

How you prepare it:

1. Combine unflavored gelatin, Lemon Jell-O, Stevia and boiling water, in large bowl and stir until gelatin has all melted.

2. Then add the ice cubes and stir until they have all melted (if using aspartame for sweetener, add it now).

3. Then add in coconut milk, coconut extract, and coconut flakes.

4. Beat with hand mixer for a minute or two until the mixture is smooth.

5. Then pour into a pretty bowl or a mold. (I put mine in one of the mini Bundt pans I just bought the other day, and it unmolded beautifully and looked really really elegant) I just dipped the bowl in hot water for 7-8 seconds and then unmolded unto a plate. Really cool looking, and tasted good too.

Egg Custard

Serves 2

Ingredients:

1 free-range egg

1 egg yolk

1 c. 1/2 and 1/2 or cream

3 tsp. sugar substitute (Stevia)

1 tsp. vanilla extract

1/8 tsp. ground nutmeg, cinnamon, or Pumpkin Pie spice

1/8 tsp. salt

How you prepare it:

1. Lightly beat the egg and yolk.

2. Add vanilla, cream, Stevia, and salt.

3. Pour into two ungreased 6 ounce custard cups.

4. Sprinkle with nutmeg. Set in a pan containing 1/2 to 1 inch of hot water.

5. Bake at 350 degrees until set for 35 minutes.

Pumpkin Custard

Serves 4

Ingredients:

5 free-range eggs

1 cup water

1 cup cream

1 tsp vanilla

4 - 6 tsp. artificial sweetener (I used Stevia, recommended)

Cinnamon and nutmeg to taste

1/2 can pumpkin

How you prepare it:

1. In blender combine the ingredients.

2. Pour in baking dish and set dish in a larger dish half filled with water.

3. Bake for 40 minutes or more until set in 350 degree preheated oven.

New York Style Cheesecake

Ingredients:

Crust (optional, I don't make a crust)

4Tbs butter softened

3pkt Equal or equivalent

1 c crushed almonds

Filling:

2 free-range eggs

3 8oz. packages Cream Cheese

2 egg whites

18 packets Equal or equivalent

1 cup sour cream

1 tsp. vanilla

2 tbsp. cornstarch

How you prepare it:

1. Preheat oven to 350.

2. Mix almonds, sweetener and butter and press into a 9 inch spring form pan evenly on bottom and 1/2 inch up on side of pan.

3. Bake until almonds are lightly toasted about 8 minutes. Cool.

4. Preheat oven to 350. Beat Cream cheese, 18 pkts Equal and vanilla until fluffy.

5. Add the free-range eggs, egg whites, cornstarch and sour cream. (I use a processor and it comes out very smooth).

6. Pour mix, over crust. Place cheesecake in pan with one inch of boiling water and bake about 45-50 minutes.

7. Remove cheesecake and cool. For a nice topping add sliced strawberries!

Yummy Orange Cheesecake

Serves 8

Ingredients:

4 free-range eggs

1 pound of cream cheese (softened)

4 tablespoons of vanilla

1 cup of cream

1/2 - 2/3 cup of Stevia (depends on how sweet you want it)

Zest of one orange OR one lemon (I've made it both way -- excellent either way)

1/4 teaspoon of salt

How you prepare it:

1. Preheat oven to 350 degrees.

2. Mix all ingredients together with a mixer until completely smooth.

3. Pour into a 10-inch pie plate (preferably glass). Bake at 350 for 25 minutes.

4. Then turn heat down to 300 degrees and bake until a knife inserted in the center comes out clean, for about 15 – 20 minutes more.

5. What I like to do is turn the oven off completely for the last five minutes, and leave the cake inside. Then take the cheesecake out and leave on counter until room temperature. Then chill. Serves 8. 4.75 grams per slices. This recipe is unbelievably yummy!

Brownie's Pumpkin Cheesecake

Serves 4

Ingredients:

3 Free-range eggs

8 packets sweet 'n low (or 1 1/2 tbsp. liquid saccharin, preferred)

8 oz. cream cheese

1/3 tsp. vanilla butter and nut flavor (with extracts in market)

1/3 tsp. vanilla extract

2 tsp. cinnamon

1 tsp. ginger

1/3 tsp. maple extract

1/2 tsp. nutmeg

1/2 can pumpkin

1/4 tsp. Lite Salt

How you prepare it:

1. Blend all ingredients in blender until liquefied.

2. Pour into 9" glass pie pan.

3. Bake at 375 degrees until it tests done with a knife, for about 30 minutes. Let cool; enjoy!

Some variations:

- You can double the recipe (only if you have a BIG food processor or blender!) pour into a deep dish pie pan and bake for 45 minutes (or tests done)

- Place a layer of pecan halves on the top before putting in the oven.

- Top with low carb whipped cream (decadent!)

- And if you can't find the fancy extracts, just use 1 tsp of vanilla.

Home-made Chocolate Pudding

Serves 2

Ingredients:

2 cups water

2 cups heavy cream

1/2 oz. baking chocolate

1/4 cup Stevia

1/2 tsp. vanilla extract

1/4 oz. unflavored gelatin

How you prepare it:

1. Put 2 cups water, in wide saucepan.
2. Sprinkle cold gelatin on water, and stir until it's all dissolved.
3. Put on stove, add all other ingredients, bring to a boil and simmer for a while, stirring constantly. (If you're using aspartame, don't add it in until later).

4. Allow to cool, then use a hand-mixer or whisk to thoroughly mix it up again. (It still tends to separate into two layers after refrigeration...)

5. Put in small bowls or cups and refrigerate thoroughly.

6. For vanilla pudding, I've used vanilla-flavored protein powder instead of the baking chocolate. Less carbohydrates, more protein that way.

Cloud 9 Chocolate Mousse

Serve 4

Ingredients:

2 tbsp. Water

4 Free-range Eggs, carefully separated

6 Packets Sweetener

1/2 cup Heavy Cream

1/2 cup Unsalted softened butter

2 oz. Unsweetened Bakers Chocolate (2 squares)

1 tbsp. Vanilla Extract

How you prepare it:

1.   Make an ice bath in a large pot. Make some boiling water in another pot.

2.   Float a smaller saucepan in the boiling water, and melt the chocolate and the 2 tbsp. water until it starts to melt.

3. Put the egg yolks in a mixer, on high, and let it run for about five minutes-
    - yolks will be light yellow and thick.

4. Add the butter to the chocolate, bit by bit, stirring constantly until you
    have a liquid goo.

5. Once the goo is nice and liquid, add the sweetener and mix it in.

6. Remove the pan from the boiling water, and put it in the ice bath, stirring
    constantly. Bring down the temperature of the chocolate until it's the same
    as your finger.

7. Slowly add the egg yolks to the chocolate mixture, mixing well. The
    mixture will curdle if you got it too hot.

8. Add in the vanilla and heavy cream. Use the hot water to warm the
    mixture (very slightly) if it begins to thicken. Set aside.

9. Completely clean your mixer, then beat the egg whites until very stiff (a
    long time).

10. Gently fold the whites into the liquid chocolate (you can use the boiling
    water to melt the chocolate if it set up while you were whipping the whites).

11. Pour mixture into four bowls, cover, chill and enjoy!

Blackberry Chiffon Pie

Serves 6

Ingredients:

1/2 cup Stevia

6 ounces fresh blackberries

1 envelope plain gelatin powder, unsweetened

1/4 teaspoon lemon oil

16 ounces softened cream cheese

Water

How you prepare it:

1.   Mix Stevia and berries, breaking berries, and let sit for half an hour.

2.   Cook berry & Stevia mixture over low heat, stirring almost continuously, until berries are completely broken and juice is released.

3.   Force through a narrow mesh sieve (or cheesecloth) to remove seeds.

4.   Measure mixture and nuke for 20 sec.

5.   Dissolve gelatin in hot berry juice and add enough cold water to bring total liquid to 2/3 cup. Mix in lemon oil.

6.   Slowly add the cream cheese and beat at slow speed. When all cream cheese has been added, beat at high speed until smooth.

7.   Blend in whipped cream, mixing at low speed.

8.   Using a spatula, scrape into the pie pan, and spread around.

9.   Chill for at least two hours.

Sugar-free Microwave Cheesecake

Serves 4

Ingredients:

Crust:

1/4 cup butter (4 Tbsp. or half of a stick)

2 Tbsp. Stevia

1 cup crushed nuts (or part nuts, part crushed All-Bran Extra Fiber cereal)

Filling:

1 pound (2 8 oz. packages) cream cheese

1 cup Stevia

1 tsp. vanilla

1/3 cup cream

4 free-range eggs

1/4 tsp salt

2 Tbsp. lemon juice (optional, I don't care for the lemon taste myself)

Topping: either 1 cup sour cream or 2 cups fresh berries

How you prepare it:

1. Put butter in microwave baking dish and microwave at High for 45 to 60 seconds until butter melts.

2. Stir in nut/cereal crumbs and sweetener.

3. Mix well and press evenly in bottom of dish.

4. Microwave at High for one and half minutes.

5. In medium mixing bowl, place cream cheese.

6. Microwave at 50% (medium) power for 1 minute or until soft.

7. Add the Stevia sweetener, salt and cream.

8. Beat at medium speed of electric mixer until blended.

9. Beat in vanilla, eggs, and lemon juice.

10. Microwave at High for 4 to 7 minutes or until very hot. (Be careful...or you'll end up cooking it in the mixing bowl). Stir and pour over crust.

11. Microwave cheesecake at 50% (Medium) power for 7 to 15 minutes, until almost set in center.

12. Cool slightly and spread with desired topping. Refrigerate at least 8 hours before serving.

Serves 6

Ingredients:

2 free-range egg

1/2 teaspoon dried oregano

4 cups cornflakes cereal

1 teaspoon garlic salt

1/4 cup all-purpose flour

1 (8 ounce) package mozzarella cheese

2 tablespoons water

How you prepare it:

1. Preheat oven to 400 degrees F (200 degrees C).

2. Lightly grease a medium baking pan lined with foil.

3. In a shallow, large bowl, crush the corn cereal to 1 cup.

4. Mix together the corn oregano, garlic salt and cereal.

5. Place the flour in a small bowl.

6. Thoroughly beat the free-range egg and water, in another small bowl.

7. Cut the mozzarella cheese into 12 sticks approximately 2 3/4 inches in length.

8. Dip the cheese sticks in the flour, then the egg mixture, then the cereal mixture.

9. Repeat dipping in the egg and cereal mixture to ensure a complete coating.

10. Arrange cheese sticks on the baking pan.

11. Allow the sticks to set for 30 minutes. Bake in the preheated oven until cheese is soft and sticks are lightly browned, about 8 minutes.

Heavenly Humus

Serves 8

Ingredients:

1 pinch paprika

1/3 cup tahini

1 tbsp. Extra-virgin olive oil

1/4 cup lemon juice

2 cloves garlic, share into half

1 tsp parsley, minced fresh

1 tsp salt

2 cups canned garbanzo beans, drained

How you prepare it:

1.   Place the tahini, garbanzo beans, lemon juice, salt and garlic in a food
      processor or blender.

2. Transfer mixture to a serving bowl, after blending until smooth.

3. Drizzle olive oil over the garbanzo bean mixture.

4. Sprinkle with paprika and parsley.

Serves 4

Ingredients:

4 cups hot air-popped popcorn

Cayenne pepper, to taste

1/2 cup freshly grated Parmesan cheese

How you prepare it

1. Toss popcorn with Parmesan and cayenne to taste.

Flavored Toasted Nuts

Serves 8

Ingredients:

1/2 cup walnuts, chopped, or nut of your choice, you can also use a mix of nuts if you want.

How you prepare it:

1. Preheat the oven to 350°F.

2. Spread the nuts out on a baking sheet.

3. Toast the nuts in the oven about 8-10 minutes, until they are lightly browned. Do NOT burn.

4. Cool and store in an airtight container for up to 2 weeks.

Pumpkin Cheesecake

Serves 6

Ingredients:

3 Free-ranges Eggs

6-8 oz. Pecans

5TB Almond Butter- melted

2 TB Stevia

4- 8oz package Philly Cream Cheese - room temp

3/4-1 cup Stevia

1/4 tsp. Ground Ginger

1/2 tsp. Cinnamon

1-15oz can Solid Pumpkin

1Tb Vanilla

How you prepare it:

1. Preheat oven to 350.
2. Crush nuts & Stevia until finely chopped.

3. Add melted butter & process until moist.

4. Press nut mixture onto bottom & 1 inch up the sides of a spring form pan.

5. Bake until golden for about 10 minutes. Cool.

6. Wrap bottom & a little up the side in double thickness tin foil.

7. Beat Stevia, cream cheese, cinnamon & ginger until smooth.

8. Add pumpkin, beat until well blended.

9. Add vanilla & eggs, beat until smooth. Pour into crust.

10. Set spring form pan into a roasting pan, fill it with hot water about an inch high.

11. Bake until top starts set & turns golden for about 1 hour & 45 minutes.

12. It's a lot of work but oh how delicious. I'm on PP so I deducted fiber from nuts & pumpkin.

Delicious Cranberry Treat

Serves 4

Ingredients:

1 cup fresh cranberries

1/2 teaspoon lemon extract

1/2 teaspoon Stevia

1/2 cup walnuts chopped

1/4 teaspoon dried orange peel

Water

How you prepare it:

1. Put washed cranberries in a pan with enough water to cover; add the rest of the ingredients except the walnuts.
2. Bring to a boil and then lower heat to simmer until it is thick.
3. Remove from heat and stir in the walnuts. Can be served warm or cold.

Serves 4

Ingredients:

For crust:

1 tsp. cinnamon

1 cup sliced almonds

2 tablespoons Almond butter.

1 packet sweetener (optional, I didn't use it)

Melt butter in pie plate. Mix the almonds, cinnamon and sweetener together with the melted butter. Press to cover pie plate.

Filling:

1 cup heavy whipping cream

1 15oz can pumpkin

2 T pumpkin pie spices or 1 tsp. each of nutmeg, cinnamon, allspice

1 box SF butterscotch Jell-O

How you prepare it:

1. Mix whipping cream and SF butterscotch Jell-O together.

2. Mix canned pumpkin with pumpkin spice in another bowl.

3. Fold the whipping cream mixture into the pumpkin mixture. Pour the whole mixture into the pie plate.

4. Chill for about 1 hr. Garnish with whip cream.

5. My almonds were 6g -3g for fiber. Whipping cream says no carbs but I don't believe it! SF butterscotch Jell-O says 6g per serving.... makes 4 servings. You'll have to do your own math depending on the type of whipping cream you use. My hubby took it to work and they loved it. They were amazed low carbing could have treats like these that tasted that good.

   I suppose you could use two boxes of butterscotch pudding if you want it sweeter. I don't have a lot of Stevia, so I'm improvising.

Marinated Veggies

"A healthy way to grill veggies! Makes a great sandwich too! "

Serves 4

Ingredients:

1/2 cup red bell pepper, sliced

1/2 cup sliced yellow bell peppers

1/2 cup zucchini, thickly sliced

1/2 cup yellow squash, sliced

16 large fresh button mushrooms

16 cherry tomatoes

1/2 cup sliced red onion

1/2 cup soy sauce

1/2 cup Extra-virgin olive oil

1/2 clove crushed garlic

1/2 cup lemon juice

How you prepare it:

1. In a large bowl, place the red bell peppers, zucchini, squash, red onion, mushrooms, yellow bell peppers, and tomatoes.

2. Combine olive oil, lemon juice, soy sauce, and garlic; mix together. Pour over the vegetables, in a small bowl.

3. Cover bowl, and marinate in the refrigerator for half an hour.

4. Preheat grill for medium heat.

5. Lightly oil grate. Remove vegetables from marinade, and place on preheated grill.

6. Cook until tender, for about 12 to 15 minutes.

There are certain foods you should avoid when you are on the grain brain diet, those foods are listed below:

Processed "gluten-free" foods

- Watch out for foods marketed and marked "gluten-free" – some of these foods are fine because they never contained gluten to begin with, but many of them are labeled as such because they have been processed, for example, ingredient such as cornmeal, cornstarch, potato starch, rice starch, or tapioca starch, have been used to replace their gluten, all of which raise blood sugar enormously; also trace amounts of gluten can remain

- Be extra cautious about gluten-free gravies, sauces, and cornmeal products – e.g. cereals, tacos, tortillas, gluten-free and corn chips

Foods containing gluten

- Oats and oat bran (unless certified gluten-free)

- Grains cracked or made into flour – bulgur (and tabbouleh), farina, graham flour, semolina

- Gluten grains – barley, kamut, triticale, rye, spelt, wheat (and wheat germ)

- Pasta, couscous, noodles – including whole-grain and whole-wheat forms
- Gluten-containing cereals
- Breads and breadcrumbs, including matzo
- Meat and dairy with gluten – blue cheeses, hot dogs, ice cream, imitation crabmeat, imitation
- Pastries and baked goods
- bacon and other imitation meats, meatballs, meatloaf, processed cheese (e.g. Velveeta), sausage
- Drinks/beverages with gluten – beer, chocolate milk (commercially prepared), instant hot drinks, flavored coffees and teas, non-dairy creamer, root beer, vodka, wheatgrass, wine coolers
- Other foods with gluten – baked beans (canned), breaded foods, cold cuts, energy bars, French fries (often dusted with flour before freezing), fried vegetables/tempura, fruit fillings and puddings, roasted nuts, seitan, soups, trail mix, veggie burgers.
- Ingredients that are often code for gluten: amino peptide complex, *Avena sativa*, brown rice syrup, caramel color (frequently made from barley), cyclodextrin, dextrin, fermented grain extract, *Hordeum distichon*, maltodextrin, *Hordeum vulgare*, hydrolysate, hydrolyzed malt extract, hydrolyzed vegetable protein,

modified food starch, natural flavoring, phytosphingosine extract, *Secale cereale*, tocopherol/vitamin E, *Triticum aestivum*, soy protein, *Triticum vulgare*, vegetable protein (HVP), yeast extract

- Pantry and condiments with gluten – bouillon/broth (commercially prepared), egg substitute, gravy, ketchup, malt/malt flavoring, marinades, mayonnaise, malt vinegar, soy sauce, teriyaki sauce, syrups, salad dressings,

Starchy vegetables

- Corn, sweet potatoes, potatoes, yams

Non-fermented soy

- Non-fermented soy foods such as tofu and soy milk

- Processed foods made with soy (look for "soy protein isolate" in the list of ingredients) – avoid soy cheese, soy burgers, soy hot dogs, soy nuggets, soy ice cream, soy yogurt

- Soy sauce containing gluten – although some naturally brewed soy sauces are technically gluten-free, many commercial brands have trace amounts of gluten – if you need to use soy sauce in your cooking, use tamari soy sauce made with 100% soybeans and no wheat

- Fruit products with high sugar levels

- Fruit juices
- Dried fruit (although dried blueberries and cranberries are included in a recipe, and prunes are listed to eat in limited quantities)
- Fried foods
- Processed fats and oils
- Margarine, vegetable shortening, trans fats
- Any commercial brand of cooking oil, even if they are organic – soybean oil, corn oil, cottonseed oil, canola oil, peanut oil, safflower oil, grapeseed oil, sunflower oil, rice bran oil, wheat germ oil, vegetable oil
- "Fat-free" and "low-fat" foods
- Packaged foods labeled "fat-free" or "low-fat" (unless they are authentically so and within the protocol, such as water, mustard, and balsamic vinegar)
- Processed carbs, sugar, and starch
- Savory – chips, crackers, cookies, pastries, muffins, pizza dough
- Sweet – cakes, doughnuts, sugary snacks, candy, energy bars, ice cream, frozen yogurt, sherbet, jams, jellies, preserves
- Drinks/beverages – sports drinks, soft drinks, soda (diet or regular)

- Pantry – chutney, ketchup, processed cheese spreads, cornstarch, cornmeal, rice starch, potato starch, tapioca starch

Sweeteners

- Natural sweeteners, including agave, honey, maple syrup (I use stevia, it is allowed in moderation)
- Processed sweeteners, including corn syrup, sugar (white and brown)

Recommended foods to reduce the risk of headaches

· Don't skip meals or keep erratic eating habits

· Watch alcohol and caffeine usage –In excess, each of these can stimulate a headache

· Go processed-, preservative-, additive-, and gluten-free

· Track the patterns of your headache experience

· Be especially careful about cured meats, aged cheese, and sources of monosodium glutamate MSG, as these ingredients may be responsible for triggering up to 30% of migraines

- Do not take caffeine after 2pm

- Avoid foods that can act as stimulants, flavorings, such as colorings, and refined carbs

- Alcohol can disrupt sleep

- Be aware of ingredients in foods that can be difficult to digest easily before going to bed – everyone will be different in this department

- Eat on a regular schedule, not erratically. This will keep your appetite hormones in check and keep the nervous system calm

- Time your dinner appropriately – find your sweet spot, leaving approximately three hours between dinner and bedtime

- Eat small portions of foods high in tryptophan, such as turkey, chicken, eggs, cottage cheese, and almonds nuts especially, as a bedtime snack. A handful of nuts might be perfect

Enjoy

If you follow religiously to <u>Dr. Perlmutter Grain Brain</u>. And some of the recipes outlined in this book. You are going to be able to boost your brain power, stay slim and smart and also have a healthy long life.

<u>If you enjoyed the recipes in this book, please take the time to share your thoughts and post a positive review with 5 star rating on Amazon, it would encourage me and make me serve you better. It'd be greatly appreciated!</u>

Other Book from the Same Author.

My 10-Day Detox Diet Cookbook: Burn the Fat, Lose weight Fast and Boost your Metabolism for Busy Mom, Restart your life with this cookbook and experience an amazing transformation of your body and your health. I am really excited for you!

CLICK HERE TO BUY: http://www.amazon.com/10-Day-Detox-Diet-Cookbook-Metabolism-ebook/dp/B00IRE3CV0

Books on Health & Fitness Diets

RECOMMENDED BOOK FOR WEIGHT LOSS AND DIET:

As Seen on T.V- Super Shred Diet Recipes: 61 Easy-to-cook Healthy Recipes To Help you Lose weight FAST in 4weeks. This Book would give you lovely Recipe Ideas for Dr. Ian Smith Super Shred Program.

CLICK HERE TO BUY:

http://www.amazon.com/dp/B00HSLGOG8

Are you looking for a Way to lose weight and keep it off for a long time while deepening your relationship with God? Then this is for you,
Get Daniel Fast Shred Diet Recipes: 35 Easy-To-Cook healthy recipes, lose 7 pounds in 7 days on the Daniel Plan. For Just $0.99 Today, for a limited Time. Lose 7 pounds in 7 days, discover the insider secret... Click on the Link below to buy Now.

http://www.amazon.com/Daniel-Shred-Recipes-Easy---Cook-ebook/dp/B00IADVBIO/

Who else wants to Experience the Incredible taste of the World's Best Sauce...?
Welcome the Brand New, Never Heard Before -The Ultimate Sriracha Hot Sauce- 25 Easy-to-Cook Healthy Recipes with This "Rooster Sauce"

CLICK HERE TO BUY:

http://www.amazon.com/dp/B00HLJWWIQ

The Pound a Day Diet Recipes: 61 easy-to-cook healthy Recipes to Help with Your Diet On A Budget...Loose that pound today eating the foods you love

Recommended for the Pound a Day Dieters

CLICK HERE TO BUY ON AMAZON:

http://bookShow.me/B00HXYU736

CPSIA information can be obtained at www.ICGtesting.com
Printed in the USA
LVOW13s1606180414

382318LV00002B/441/P